T0196461

*She*
## Smiles
*and*
## Cries

# She
# *Smiles*
## and
# *Cries*

## Reflections 1

Inshirah Aleem

authorHOUSE®

*AuthorHouse™*
*1663 Liberty Drive*
*Bloomington, IN 47403*
*www.authorhouse.com*
*Phone: 1-800-839-8640*

*Published by AuthorHouse    04/24/2012*

*ISBN: 978-1-4685-9567-3 (sc)*
*ISBN: 978-1-4685-9566-6 (e)*

# Dedication

This book is for all the teenagers who have given up on life . . . You are not alone.

For: Nisaa . . .You are my light—my inspiration . . . Mommy loves you more!

# Contents

# Introduction

## Who I Am

*Inshirah (The Expansion of the Breast or Heart)*
*Surah 94: Holy Quran*

*In the Name of Allah, Most Gracious, Most Merciful*
*Have we not*
*Expanded you your breast (heart)?*
*And removed from you*
*Your burden*
*The which did gall your back*
*And raised high the esteem*
*In which you are held*
*So, verily with every difficulty*
*There is relief*
*Verily, with every difficulty*
*There is relief*
*Therefore, when you are Free (from your immediate task)*
*Still labor hard*
*And to your lord*
*Turn all your attention*

I was named after a surah or chapter in the Qur'an entitled *Inshirah*. My name is a reminder that life promises us struggle with relief and we are given no burden greater than what our heart can bear.

I am a Muslim, someone who submits their will to Allah, our Creator. I am a person who loves life; I accept the ups and downs and the humility it takes to endure the things we cannot control.

I am a believer—a believer in the purity and beauty of all religions. I am a fighter—a fighter who believes that growth cannot occur without struggle and life does not evolve without growth.

I believe we are all unique prisms of light; however, mental illness can come along and darken our hopes and dreams—turning diamonds into blackened stones. We all have to find our way on the road to recovery. Sharing my story is my way. It is a reminder of the light that will shine despite the darkness felt in the challenging times. At the end of the day, whatever "way" YOU find, remember there is always a way.

This is easier said than done. This is especially true on those days when you have to fight yourself to get out of the bed, or those days when you have to fight your thoughts in order to get through the day. I have been there. I call 'those' days the eye of the storm, and they will eventually end just like every storm ends . . . leaving the sunlight to follow.

My story is not only for those who deal with mental illness. It is for anybody who suffers from hardship and we all do. My life is a story of triumph because after all I have been through, I am still here. I am here praying my words will make a difference in your lives, praying you will find your way . . .

# Part One

## Invasion . . .

# A Struggle Through Time

I was 14
Prime of my time
Head to the sun
Knew it all
Had it all
15
Whole world is shaken
Time is all the Same now
No Hours—No Minutes—No Seconds
Misery is present
I am Sick
Not physically
Mentally
My mind is invaded
Attacked
Desecrated
And Me
I am a walking corpse
Trying to find a piece of peace
Struggle making me stronger
I am surviving
With each day
With each trial
I am surviving
From 14-15-to now
From Seconds-Minutes-to Hours
I have found the pieces
I have found MY peace

*I wish I could hold her hand, walk through this time with her, reassure her, and tell her our Creator will never leave her, and will never let her down. I'd tell her she will be back from this dark space; I'd tell her she will be back to live and breathe refreshing happiness and in the moments of unrelenting fear and pain . . . I wish I could take the fear that churns my stomach even now away . . . but I can't. She will have to walk this path alone in order for "she" to be me.*

You could have hit me upside my head, pulled out every single strand of hair on my head, and lit me on fire and I would have been unaware of it all. My mind was detached from awareness leaving my body unable to function. I could not eat on my own, walk on my own, and I was verbally unresponsive. I have no memories of this time, no memories of my own . . . only an "after" understanding—an understanding that I was sitting in the juvenile psych ward. The year was 1992 and there were multiple raised brows and deepening creases on the foreheads of the doctors who were reviewing my case.

My condition was rare, but words of optimism easily flowed from the doctor's mouth to my parents, "She will be okay, Mr. and Mrs. Aleem. We will bring your daughter back to you." The unspoken reality was staring them all in their faces, the reality of me: listless, a shadow of an existence, a screaming whisper of the truth ringing louder and louder. No one really knew if I'd come back, and if I come back what kind of life I would have. I was a special case.

# Rebirth

**I**NSHIRAH
**N**eeds God's Inspiration to
**S**truggle through
**H**er unwanted demons that
**I**gnite a pain which
**R**uns
**A** wave throughout her tainted
**H**EART


    I was out of it for about 30 days. My first memories connected to the absence are currents of unrelenting and yielding torment. I was emerging in a paranoid state of psychosis, which means I was still detached from reality but knew enough to know the fear that enveloped my consciousness.


I hear footsteps, voices . . .
I feel my heart beating rapidly . . . the footsteps are coming
    for me . . . are coming to hurt me. . . no faces, no
    names . . . just whispers . . .
I am crying.
I am shaking with fear, the footsteps are closer . . . the voices
    are louder . . .
I cry out.
I scream out for my mother.
I call out for Allah, cry for Him.
I hear footsteps, voices . . .
I feel my heart beating rapidly . . .
I am crying.
I am shaking.
I am screaming.

My mother, she is brushing my hair, singing soothing words settling my fears . . .

My mother, she is singing, "Allah is truly amazing, Allah is truly amazing." I can feel her . . . Allah . . . her warmth . . . His Warmth . . . her love . . . His love . . . I want to smile, but consciousness leaves me.

I am in a room. I have a plate of food in front of me, and a frail young woman next to me. A glass window is facing me and my parents are on the other side. The nurse is there and has a whole bunch of pills. They are multi-colored and some are big as heck. She says open up and I do. I swallow all of the pills; seems like I am swallowing forever, seems like I am swallowing hundreds of pills. I feel groggy . . . look up at my parents and close my eyes.

**Reality Check #1:**

The pill scenario: Real.
My mother singing: Real.
The people coming to hurt me: My Real.
The fear, the crying, and screaming: My Real.

**My Real**: If you were looking at me physically, you might have seen me whimpering and moaning—body shaking. My mind was barely there—captured in a never ending nightmare. The people coming to hurt me, my screams for help . . . not real but all too real. They would get so close, over and over again, same voices, same whispers . . . they would always leave though . . . never get so close that I could see them. It was like a gun was being pointed at my head and the trigger was being pulled in a deadly game of Russian Roulette.

I don't know what day in the absence everything occurred. I do know the more complete memories reflect a more complete me. I was fighting my way through . . . pushing through to reality.

It is not easy writing about this time. There are empty holes in my mind between what I "thought" and what really was. They say every three seconds a person is born. On day 30, in one second, I was reborn and everything was new. I knew how to walk and eat and I knew people's names. I didn't know myself though . . . I didn't know my mind. I tried to connect the holes in my memory, but my mind wouldn't allow me to dig too deep for too long. Self preservation. I was safe in the present and wanted to remain that way.

Post-partum. I was hospitalized and unable to go home for what seemed like a decade, but was really about another month. The barred windows housed me in a juvenile psych ward where doctors, meds, Occupational Therapy (OT) and group counseling governed my day.

During my multiple month stay, my diagnosis was complete . . . a severe form of Bipolar Disorder, which back then was solely referred to as Manic Depression. The diagnosis did not come easily. Most of the doctors never saw a break so severe in a person so young in the early 90s. Even now, most people with Bipolar have major breaks over the age of eighteen. On top of that, it was basically unheard of back then for people with Manic Depression to have hallucinations.

The hardest part for me was losing my mind. The physically and mentally unresponsive state I experienced stole my memories, my time and a part of me changing my life forever. The medicine—all of those pills—required to bring me "back" diminished my quality of life with harsh side effects. It was the struggle of my life to fight for vitality once I had a severe break from reality. It has been the struggle of my life.

After the diagnosis, it was treatment plan time.

Doctors: You will need to be medicated with around 27 pills a day accompanied with intense counseling for the rest of your life, or you will lose your mind again. (Not exact words)

Me: Or I will lose my mind again? (Then came the disclaimer)

Doctors: (The "full" disclaimer that they never "really" gave because they never "really" knew) If you are on these medicines you will gain over one hundred pounds, you will be debilitated by lethargy on a daily basis, you will have eye seizures, spasms, your hair will fall out, your kidneys and liver may lose functioning, you will have hand tremors, muscle stiffness and the quality of your life will be so close to death that you might as well die. But you will never have to be that sick again. And one more thing, you will have to be on all of these meds for the rest of your life . . . So . . . how does that make you feel?

As life and death hung in the balance and the line between them was skewed and distorted . . .
I said . . .
I'm just glad I never have to be that sick again . . .

**Reality Check #2:**

Of course, this did not happen exactly in this manner. There was a meeting and some of the possible side effects of the medicine were presented to me. They did ask me if I approved of the treatment plan, which I might add made no sense to me back then. I was a minor and my parents already signed off on the treatment. On top of that, the doctors asked me as if I had the power to say no to what the doctors never "really" knew. Essentially, they were asking permission from me for me to be okay with living as the walking dead.

# Part Two

## Hidden Fractures

You hear it all the time—especially with siblings—the different perspectives at the same time in the same family. Sometimes, it is like you are hearing about a different family depending on who you speak with. What we remember shapes the different perspectives, and the memories we hold onto dictate how we progress in life.

I choose these examples from my childhood to navigate you through specific experiences that influenced my broken identity. My childhood was more good than bad, but these are the seeds rooted in me . . . distorting my self-perception, and setting the stage for my future breakdown.

I remember being told I was spoiled—the center of attention. The youngest girl of four, the baby, I was told I got away with murder half the time. I don't remember the unhinged freedom. I do remember feeling lonely and out of place.

I remember getting on my bike, and not telling anybody and pedaling myself to nowhere but everywhere. I felt free in flight. I'd end up at friends or family. To everybody else, I was running away and I guess they were right. I would just leave. To me, I felt the safest running away. I felt like I was running to something versus away from something.

I remember my sisters used to tell me that I was running away to get more attention. That's not how I felt. I felt like I was running away to get away from the attention—the good and bad. I remember being teased about my weight and feeling so hurt by it. I remember being praised because I was so smart with a pretty face and wondering why it mattered so much. I remember feeling more than thinking and I ran to feel—I ran-to feel safe.

I remember people making an awful big deal out of the length and texture of my hair—naturally curly ringlets that traveled down my back. "Your hair is so long. Where did you get that Indian hair? You must got Indian in your family girl," so the choir sang. The better for me was always my face and hair. The worse for me was always my weight.

I was in tuned with feeling the good, the bad and the ugly in life at a very young age and held onto all of it . . . I was in tuned, but also imbalanced with how I perceived myself in this life. I was too good or not good enough. I was too pretty or not pretty enough, and I tried to run away from all of it. All of these feelings ran deep within me, and were not easily escaped.

# A Picture of Me Leaving Me

*Parents: You are going to have to leave . . . This will be your last year.*

*Me: Nothing.*

*Parents: Your father and I cannot afford it.*

*Me: Nothing.*

*Parents: Your sisters are going to college and they cut your scholarship . . . we just can't afford . . .*

*Me: Nothing*

*I wonder what they were looking at when they told me I could no longer attend my precious private school. They of course were looking at me, but I wonder what I looked like . . . my facial expression. I can tell you how I felt . . . I felt like nothing.*

Leaving my private school freshman year, I was leaving a future I never had. I was going to be this great lawyer. I was going to go to Harvard and have this great life with a great car and tons of money. I left this future and was sent into a present past of misery. I was sent to a local public high school for my sophomore year. The tenth grade class was the size if not bigger than my old school's entire student body. I remember feeling swallowed up by the size of the school alone. I was unprepared for how it would, by design, chew me up and spit me out.

Old School versus New School Lunch: We had a dining room with couches and a dessert bar—privileges that most do not get to entertain. We talked about the latest news, we laughed and laughed some more, and sometimes sang and danced right in the middle of our dining room palace . . . I step into the dirty white-walled, brown-tabled, cold lunch room at my new school with eyes peering at me and not a comfy couch in sight. I quickly look down and find myself nowhere to sit in a corner, in a huge lunch room of kids laughing and enjoying life . . . that was me, I remember telling myself, that was me. As I looked around me, I quickly realized the past tense was attacking my present sense of being.

New School Lunch: I began skipping lunch all together. It was just me and the bathroom. For months, it was just me in the bathroom, crying, pulling my legs up on the toilet seat, tight to my chest, just in case someone sees and then crying some more . . .

# If You dumb yourself down you will be liked

*Well, this is what I subconsciously told myself and it worked to an extent. I repeat . . . to an extent. It was a dance I played with myself but was really playing myself.*

Most teenagers feed off of what others feel and think. For an example, you tell an adolescent that they will be dumb and amount to nothing enough times they will believe that they are dumb and they will amount to nothing. I was not equipped with the heart to handle all that people thought of me and threw at me. Seeds of self-doubt were already planted as a youth and at my new school they festered, they grew, they devoured my sanity . . .

## My Message:

I was stuck up . . . long hair to prove that.
I was a know it all . . . honor classes and a clever tongue to prove that.
I was too fat . . . my grandest weakness, easily displayed, and easily attacked.

## My Reaction:

I believed the worst of what they saw in me and became whatever people thought of me.

# Part Three

## The (Im)possible(s)

# Captive

*I am captive, drowning rapidly*
*I am a prisoner of my dreams*
*The truth never being what it seems*
*My passions cry out wanting to be free*
*Pain is an obstruction haunting me*
*While trials to purify my soul clean*
*Are disillusioned by wasted means*
*Survival has curtailed my reality*
*I am prisoner of deception*
*Left alone to cry*
*I am a captive of perceptions*
*Trapped with questions of why*
*I am slowly sinking pulled by bait*
*While time for me, will not wait*

# Dumbing me Down

*It was quite easy, really.*

I grew up surrounded by predominately girls, my old school was all girls so when boys were thrown into the equation, my descent naturally accelerated, but for all the wrong reasons. I disowned everything I was proud of: my intelligence, my family values, and my belief system. I became "that" girl—the girl that everybody hates to love 'cause the boys love to love her . . . and the dance with the devil begins.

I was stuck up; I flaunted my long hair to show it. I was a know it all; I made sure my clever tongue never let me down. I was "the good girl gone bad", and the boys loved me.

I spent too much time focusing on my looks, flipping my hair and switching my hips; I was completely incomplete. If anyone called me fat, like a record, I'd play the part of not caring. I'd lie to myself and tell me that they were ALL jealous. I began lying to everybody and the lies multiplied and multiplied and multiplied.

I would lie convincingly with a smile or frown on my face depending on the part I had to play. I would skip school, smoke weed and lie some more. I lied so much I started to believe my own lies. I'd engage in reckless sexual behavior and lie some more. My thoughts would race to fight each other and sleep evaded me in the midst of an uncontrollable battle.

ME: . . . didn't do an assignment, I'd tell my teacher that my grandmother was sick and I was at the hospital all night.

ME: . . . she has been a bit ill lately. Who cares about the stupid assignment anyway?

ME: . . . steal jewelry from family and friends and boldly deny it while wearing the very item I stole.
ME: . . . it is on me, right? It is mine. I don't even know what they talkin' bout.

ME . . . smoke weed with a whole bunch of guys and fake like I was living the Bonnie and Clyde thug life.
ME: I don't even know how to inhale this S***. Oh well, I look good smoking it.

ME: . . . have make out sessions with my boyfriend in front of anybody and anywhere.
ME: The light of consciousness glows. My mind quiets long enough to allow the flood of tears to flow . . .

And in the end, the promise of tears would always win . . .

**Reality Check #3:**

Bipolar manifests into phases defined as Mania and Depression. My Mania caused the sleepless nights/insomnia, uncontrollable thoughts/mind-racing, reckless behavior/ impaired judgment (sex, lying, drugs and stealing). What I have described so far has mainly been my Mania with a small taste of Depression, which always took over and became present with uncontrollable sadness, anxiety, feelings of worthlessness, shame and guilt. This was *my* Bipolar Disorder.

*My* onset (first episode of Bipolar) occurred over a year's time span without treatment, which influenced the severity of symptoms. Essentially, the hallucinations and catatonic state may not have occurred if I received proper treatment earlier on. I emphasize "*my*" because every person is different. This is an important part to humanizing the disease. Not every teenager with Bipolar goes through the same thing. Not every adult with Bipolar goes through the same thing. This also makes diagnosis difficult at times.

For me, the very symptoms that I was going through mirrored a "troubled" teenager who was having a difficult transition time at a new school. There are many teenagers who go through tough stages—many teenagers have sex—many teenagers lie. It wasn't until I became depressed my parents saw that I needed help and they tried to help. They brought me to the psychologist and I would lie to the doctor . . . not mention the sleepless nights, the mind-racing, the lying, the stealing . . . I believed that I was just going through a tough time right now and no one needed to know how tough time really was right now. My Mania created a world of make-believe that fooled everyone including myself. It was impossible for my parents to know what was wrong with me . . . until the "impossible(s)" happened.

# The Impossible:
# My Last Stand

*Running away—like a caged animal to be—running nowhere but from the beast in me.*

Towards the end of the breakdown period, I began running away habitually. The last time I ran away, the police became involved, and I had to go to court. Sitting in court, I no longer recognized myself; this person who lies to her friends and family; this person who steals from her friends and family. I needed a way out. I needed to go . . . to leave . . . So I declared to the court that I wanted to divorce my family and go into foster care.

The dramatic declaration just erupted . . . no thought process involved. I remember taking on my father's (my mother was not with me) twister of rage and hurt. He started yelling at me. He was screaming at me. If only he knew I was yelling and screaming at me more, but no one knew. I barely knew what was going on with me. All I knew was the shame that pulled me in tortured directions. "This person" didn't deserve their love. "This person" was plagued with fear and hatred . . . self-hatred. I wanted my parents to stop me . . . to make the worry, the sleepless nights, the crying, the stealing, the sex, the uncontrollable thoughts . . . to make it all go away, but they had no idea. They let me go and I wanted them to, but really didn't want to go . . .

# Foster Care and Happy Ever Never Land

*It wasn't the best of places. It wasn't the worst of places.*

Trash bags were my dressers. I slept in bunk beds with other foster care children. I called my mother every day crying and begging to come home. Even as I was crying to go home, the greater part of me felt like I had no right to go home. I was a tortured soul.

**Turning Point**: I went to the mall with my foster care family and lo and behold—guess who was there? My sisters . . . they call after me . . . "Shirah, Shirah!" I turn towards them and in a flash have a moment of clarity . . . I realize how much I **HAD** to be with them . . . to be with my family . . . to be home . . . but where was home?

No matter how lost you become . . . home is where your doubts and fears are grounded. I now see home is in the light of the Creator, but this revelation comes with the glow of hindsight. I was a fifteen year-old ghost of a person who was losing her soul—her connection to a Higher Power. Home was anywhere I didn't have to face myself. Darkness was my home.

# Coming Home and
# Losing Forever

*My reality*
*I see the beast that lives in me*
*Beating me wholly*
*but not really*

Foster Care was over. Bonds were paid to the court and I was sent home. The process happened quicker than expected and quite simply. The entire "foster care" experience was a little over a month. Later, I learned my parents kept me there longer to teach me a lesson. I remember feeling like I deserved the lesson and feeling redeemed because it was a lesson learned. When I first saw my mother, I ran into her loving arms. I cried and yearned for her warmth to fill me up whole . . . a humanly impossible task.

Once home, things appeared to be going so much better. I had to go to summer school but essentially did just enough to skate by tenth grade with a passing average. Mind you, I spent the majority of the year skipping so I was pretty amazed with how I was able to skate. Then, just like that, I was struck and landed in a completely new world.

It started with a feeling. My father was late picking me up from summer school one day. So I decided to walk home. It was a pretty far walk home, but I couldn't wait. This feeling in me forced me to go. During the walk, I felt eyes were watching me in disapproval. I would look at people and see them shaking their heads in a false reality. A sense grew in me that I was no longer going home . . . that this world I was walking in was no longer my world.

I would look at people and they would nod their heads to me as if they knew what I was questioning. A great sense of paranoia held me in an inescapable place. I was paying for all the sins I committed. I was tormented by the knowing eyes, by this feeling and soon I believed what my new world was telling me . . . this was my Hell.

I stopped taking showers.

I was going to be late for summer school. I could barely move. I remember my parents shouting at me to take a shower and I just couldn't. My mother grabbed my arm and pulled me into the shower. I just stood there. I knew enough to know that she was mad. I knew enough to know that a haze was slowly descending upon me and I could do nothing about it . . . I couldn't move even though I wanted to . . . I was so scared but felt like I was no longer in control . . . I went to school, but felt like I was being pulled there . . . I was no longer myself . . . the paranoia grew . . . the darkness grew and I knew . . . I knew I was losing this battle.

I stopped recognizing who people were.

I was going to the store with my mother and a woman we hadn't seen in a while stopped us and gave me a great big hug. For the life of me, I couldn't remember her and I couldn't hug her back. I just stood there blank. My mother thought I was being rude . . . I was scared because every part of me wanted to react . . . to act happy to see this woman who was happy to see me, but I couldn't . . . I just couldn't. The haze was overpowering me, and even though I couldn't move I felt like I was falling . . . falling into its powerful pull.

I stop seeing reality.

There is a plastic dinner container rattling in the refrigerator. I hear it from my bedroom. I jump up. The noise startles me and I run to see it. The container is shaking wildly. I cry for my mom to open up the container. She rushes in the kitchen, just as she opens the container, the rattling stops and there it is—a possum. But it isn't alive. In front of me is a blood-stained container that holds a dead and disfigured possum . . . I scream louder than humanly possible.

I feel them . . . animals . . . in me . . . Snakes . . . Alligators . . . More of the same . . . I touch my arms . . . I touch my legs . . . I touch my stomach and feel them . . . see them move in serpent like patterns . . .

. . . And then—just like that— there is nothing . . .

Only an 'after' understanding . . .

**Reality Check #4:**

There are more memories. There were more hallucinations. The ones that I have mentioned are the ones that have stuck with me. I remember my connection to life quickly dissolving. By the time I felt the reptiles, I did not have the strength to yell or scream out. I would touch them and feel numb. I was losing it and I remember bits and pieces of my descent but don't care to remember for too long.

My parents tell me I was hallucinating and talking about being in Hell for a couple of weeks before my mind and then body shut down. I often wondered what took them so long to get me help and I eventually asked. They thought I was playing around, seeking attention with the hallucinations. They had just suffered a year of me playing around and bringing me in for help and getting nowhere. So they assumed the worst, which is the stage I set for myself. It wasn't until I stopped talking and walking they knew I needed professional help. Everything happened very quickly . . . they did the best they could do with a whole bunch of (im)possible(s) . . .

# Part Four

## You Will Never Have to Be that Sick Again . . .

# Stained

*Do you understand me?*
*Feel my Pain*
*Or are you afraid to see*
*This pain that has left your stain*
*This pain hidden in me*
*Preventing me to feel*
*The only thing that is real*
*Do you understand me?*
*Feel my pain*
*Or are you afraid to see*
*This pain that has left your stain*
*This pain that beckons me to kneel*
*Preventing me to feel*
*The only thing that is real*
*My stain*
*Your pain*
*My pain-begging me to kneel*
*Or maybe it's me who cannot deal?*


## Integration . . .

I spent a summer (three months) of being slowly integrated back to "normal" world. The barred windows, daily counseling, and Occupational Therapy that governed my day, soon became filled with daily visits home. Daily visits home, turned into leaving the hospital forever. Leaving the hospital forever, turned into a day program at another site with partial-day counseling back to normal world.

It was eventually time for me to return to school. "This time was going to be different" was my family's reoccurring theme. I was anxious and scared and held onto my theme, "you will never have to be that sick again." I took all my pills—even the big as heck ones. I went to individual counseling and wanted to get better. I was afraid of losing my mind again and did whatever I had to do to make sure I was safe. I held onto as many pieces of me as possible . . . just enough to truly be okay.

## Too Hard to Get . . .

It wasn't easy sitting in a planned meeting—organizing a planned friendship to protect me from loneliness. This time was going to be different (the reoccurring theme presenting itself once again). This time we are all prepared, they told me. Smaller school . . . familiar . . . my sisters went there. It will be better . . . they all appeared to feel better about 'this time' . . . they all were . . . but me.

It wasn't easy walking into my first lunch and waiting for my arranged friendship to save me. It wasn't easy coming home . . . looking at the expectant faces expecting me to break. It wasn't easy recognizing that pieces of me were cut too small to break. I should have been grateful for all the preemptive preparation . . . grateful and hopeful. A part of me was . . . a part of me held onto scattered pieces of hope: soft whispers that told me maybe this time will be different, but they were *scattered* pieces . . . just within beyond my reach.

## Salvation . . . .

The planned meeting actually worked. I remember being saved by the arranged friendship and many more friendships at my new high school. I forgot how good it felt to laugh. I forgot how liked I was . . . how funny I could be . . . how people naturally gravitated toward me. I told myself I was going to be the perfect friend. The major problem with trying to be a perfect friend is that no one is perfect. I had unrealistic expectations for others and myself.

I remembered if my friend gave another friend more attention I would purposefully do things like not talk to my friend as a way of getting back at her, or if a friend made a mistake and did something human like forget to call me, I would not speak to them for weeks. While everyone was going along on a normal curve of development, I was a sixteen "two" year old, post-partum, and I struggled with social interactions. There was also the fear that I would be alone again with no friends, so I clung to the idea that I had to be the best friend, and the perfect friend to everybody. This distorted what I tolerated from my "so called" friends.

When someone wronged me on the normal curve of development, like used me or lied to me, I assumed it was me who could have done something differently. "I" didn't matter; instead, having friends was more important and being the perfect friend was my way to keep them . . . my twisted, humanly impossible goal . . .

I remember being saved from boys—not in a healthy way. As the scale started heading up past the 250 mark, the girl who girls loved to hate because the boys loved to love her was being swallowed by her weight. I was just cute enough to hang with the cutest girls in school, but not cute enough to be liked by the cutest guys in school. My fragile ego was stung by the bitter rejection. But I figured if I had my girls and was no longer 'that sick anymore' . . . The "guy thing" was just a scattered piece that I was happy to be out of reach as I was gathering myself whole. Despite my conviction, as I tried to hold on, feelings of worthlessness forced me to let go.

# Suicide

*Sometimes I'm mad at my father*
*Sometimes I'm mad at my mother*
*Sometimes I'm mad at my sisters*
*Sometimes I'm mad at nobody*
*And most times . . . most times*
*I'm mad at myself*

It was a beautiful, warm summer day. The summer before my senior year. The kinda' day where the breeze carries you.

He was a friend of a friend who had been checking me out for a while.

We did "it".

When it was all over he put my name on the wall.

I was his conquest, etched in black marker across the wall.

I was the girl who let a guy she barely knew do her in a basement.

I walked to the grocery store.

Called my parents to come get me.

Told them what I did.

Told them exactly how nasty I felt.

Cried until my puffy eyelids hovered over my burning eyes.

Couple hours later . . . I took enough pills to make the shame go away . . . to make me go away.

I tried to kill myself because I didn't want to feel anything anymore because I felt unworthy of any caring. My parents found the empty bottles and rushed me off to the hospital.

The doctors gave me liquefied charcoal, which I can plainly say tasted like the worst thing I have ever tasted in my life. I had to swallow about three cups. The charcoal solidified the pills, preventing them from permeating my blood stream just enough to keep me alive . . .

At the hospital, I was blessed with the same doctors who knew the history and labeled this an acute, minor, episode. I always felt so weird; almost like I didn't deserve the illness that excused my sins. I couldn't help it . . . it didn't seem just that my sexual transgressions were a symptom of my Bipolar. But I didn't know what the "appropriate" justice looked like . . . 'cause I just felt so lost. The sex was one of many symptoms. I focused on the sex because it created a presence of shame that no amount of pills could cure. The doctors gave me more pills to help with all the symptoms, and I was released in less than a month's time . . . I took the pills without question and with no hesitation because the fear of being 'that sick again' was a stain that ran synonymous with hope.

**Reality Check #5:**

The suicide attempt was a surprise for my family. I had spent the last years in school somewhat adjusting with friends and being happy and "things were better this time." So when I did what I did and then tried to take my life, everyone was surprised. It was hard for people to understand that there were times I faked the happiness. I played the part of being okay because I really wanted to be, but there were times I really wasn't even when I fought my hardest. It was a constant battle when the anxiety, sadness, and other symptoms plagued my existence. You see, the pills controlled the symptoms but failed to erase them. There was also the trauma of having hallucinations and being in a catatonic state. I was scared of the before time when I lost my mind, and the fear followed me into my present, attacking my hopes for the future.

*One Pill,*

    *Two Pill,*

        *Three Pill,*

        *Four,*

            *Five Pill,*

                *Six Pill . . .*

                    *21 Pills more*

I was doing better after the suicide attempt and was preparing myself for my senior year, which was a whole other beast. I appeared to be stable and was as stable as I could be . . .

By the time doctors became comfortable with my progress no doctor felt secure enough to take away even some of the pills. My parents definitely didn't feel safe enough to ask the doctors to take away some of the pills. So I was stuck on 27 pills a day . . . faced to deal with the side effects that worsened with time.

Senior year was the height of the worst. I would fall asleep in class all of the time, and go to the nurse's office to sleep the tired away only to wake up and feel more tired. Eventually, with the simple shuffle of papers, I was allowed to be home-schooled . . . allowed to do my school work from school at home so I could graduate because everyone knew the likelihood of me graduating was unlikely as I slept the days away . . .

The salvation I found in friendships quickly slipped away. I was becoming more lethargic and less "fun." Being my friend became a job that most young and spry teenagers didn't sign up for . . . I was, once again, alone. But I was used to the feeling and the pills made me forget the loneliness. They were there with me . . . my worst enemy . . . best reminder that I lived through worst times.

Side Effects (some of the many): The pills would make my hands shake to the point where holding a cup, bottle or any object made a rattling noise and became a testy challenge. The pills would make it so hard to go to the bathroom that I would cry at times when trying to make a bowel movement. As the pills stayed, my thyroid became damaged, which meant that I was not metabolizing the food I was eating, which meant that I was hitting the scale close to the 330 lbs mark.

I couldn't fit into seat belts found in the average car. I couldn't fit into most clothes. Even the stores for big people didn't carry my size of clothing, which by then was 30/32. My feet were so swollen that I couldn't wear "normal" shoes. We would go out to eat as a family and I wouldn't be able to fit in the booths. We would go to the doctors and they all were concerned with what would happen to me if they took me off the pills. So I was fixed in an impossible hole . . . being held by too many pills. But in the back of my mind there was my reoccurring theme, 'I never had to be that sick again,' and my reoccurring theme remained true. So I stayed immobilized by 27 pills, but mobile enough to smile at the truth.

And in the end . . .

I graduated.

I accomplished what many thought I'd never do . . . I graduated despite the weight of the side effects . . . despite the weight of the fear and the uncertainty of the past found in my present. It was far from easy. I didn't simply smile my way to graduation. I didn't simply smile my way to the clothing stores that never had my clothing size. I didn't simply smile my way through all the side effects. In fact, I cried most of the time and begged . . . I begged the Creator to make it all better . . . to make the symptoms and side effects go away. So, no, it wasn't easy to smile. It was even harder to believe in my smiles, but in my mind I had no choice.

It was all very logical to me. Just as I didn't have to break at such a young age, I did not have to come back . . . that was my reason for pushing myself. The Creator brought me back for a reason, and I believed in Him . . . believed that every time I cried there was a reason to smile. I believed in the meaning of my name, with every difficulty there is relief, and there was always some type of relief . . . seen in my family who became my anchor and gave me precious gems of joy to hold onto when I wanted to let go of everything. So I was immobilized by 27 pills, but mobile enough to smile my way through . . . to smile *my way* through.

# You Can't Stop My Shine

*I wish I could write a different script*
*One where I believe in me*
*And trust the Creator*
*Using His love as an elevator*
*To elevate to a higher level*

*I wish I could write a different script*
*One Where I am whole*
*Not sliced to pieces*
*Unable to see my choices*

*I wish I could write a different script*
*One where I am able to see pass the darkness*
*That blackens my heart and soul*
*Making me inhuman*
*Making me unfit*
*So I can fit into a cancerous mold*

*Why do I create my destiny*
*based on a history*
*of lies I told*
*I am the beauty I stole*

*I am the Queen*
*The Warrior*
*The Conqueror*
*The anything*
*and the everything*
                *And I Can't Forget*
                *And I Won't Forget*
*I CAN write a different script*

# Epilogue
## Leaving the sunlight to follow . . .

I have known for quite some time that my purpose in life is to write about my illness and share my struggles and triumphs. I have always been proud of how I continue to conquer and own my illness. It, however, hasn't always been easy for me to share my story with self-doubt shadowing my awareness, darkening the stigma attached to mental illness. I started to gain more resolve when I heard the outlandish stereotypes being pumped throughout the media and people repeating them as if they were the only truths.

The misconception that people with Bipolar are often homicidal and violent towards others is common and very damaging. **The truth**: there are several different symptoms associated with the Bipolar illness and homicidal behavior is not one of them. **The truth**: people with Bipolar *sometimes* display reckless behavior, which can range from impulsive shopping to promiscuity. **The truth:** a person can be violent, irrational and homicidal without an illness to scapegoat.

Another common misconception is that people with Bipolar get mad for no reason and are happy in one moment and angry in the next. **The truth**: the "bi-polar" or two phases that can be misconstrued as creating this type of behavior are defined as Mania and Depression. **The truth**: specific behavior is associated with each phase, and occurs over periods of time and not in split moments. **The truth:** a person can be happy, sad, angry and emotional without an illness to scapegoat.

**The undeniable truth:** I have reached a milestone in completing this book and I can say without a doubt that no one and nothing can stop me from believing Bipolar is my gift that I will always have, but will never have me . . .

So what is to come? *Reflections 2* with more of my struggles with weight, debilitating side effects, coming off the 27 pills, and how I overcame what some may argue to be insurmountable hurdles. But, I am still here and what is life without struggle? No life . . .

# Special Thanks

First and always, I thank Allah (the Creator) of all things. Since my late twenties, I have been blessed with remission, which has caused the disappearance of my most taxing symptoms. Bipolar Remission is when symptoms disappear or become significantly reduced for a prolonged period of time. It is not promised to everyone with Bipolar Disorder. This is a lifelong illness, and I have been blessed with the proper treatment and support systems that have allowed me to stay in remission. My doctors often said the reason why I healed and became so successful was because I had a supportive family. They have loved me through it all, and I am here today largely in part to their collective efforts.

Daddy, I love you so much. You have worked so hard and sacrificed so much for me to have a successful life. You once told me nothing in life worth having comes easy. Those words have helped me to find my way. Mom, you are my anything and everything on Earth. You are a light to so many people and I admire your strength and compassion. I am the woman I am because of you.

If you or a loved one is experiencing any of the following symptoms of Bipolar Disorder for a prolonged period of time (usually two or more weeks), please go seek medical treatment. Below, you will also find hotline numbers for anyone who is having suicidal thoughts or desires.

**Common Symptoms for Bipolar Disorder (Mania):**
Feeling unusually "high" and optimistic **or** extremely irritable
Unrealistic, grandiose beliefs about one's abilities or powers
Sleeping very little, but feeling extremely energetic
Talking so rapidly that others can't keep up
Racing thoughts; jumping quickly from one idea to the next
Highly distractible, unable to concentrate
Impaired judgment and impulsiveness
Acting recklessly without thinking about the consequences
Delusions and hallucinations (in severe cases)

**Common Symptoms for Bipolar Disorder (Depression):**
Feeling hopeless, sad, or empty
Irritability
Inability to experience pleasure
Fatigue or loss of energy
Appetite or weight changes
Sleep problems
Concentration and memory problems
Feelings of worthlessness or guilt
Thoughts of death or suicide

***National Suicide Prevention Lifeline*:** 1-800-273-**TALK** (8255), available 24/7 and free

***National Adolescent Suicide Hotline*:** 1-800-621-4000

# Within

*I picked up my pen*
*Aspirations of bringing a message*
*From within*
*Through my soul*
*I begin*

*Who I Am*
*Wanting to make a difference*
*Sending a message*
*Giving a lesson*
*Communication is my vessel to grow*

*I continue . . .*
*What is within me*
*A brain heart and soul*
*A combination of struggle antagonizing . . .*
*Who I Am*

*I continue . . .*
*I write from a point in my past*
*where my mental conception begins*
*with the pen and pad as my friends*

*Ever heard of that phrase*
*I once was blind but now . . . I'm free*
*That is the feeling coming over me*
*Possessing me*
*Taking me on a ride*
*With the pen and pad as my guide*

*I was afraid to use them*
*My faculties*
*Afraid to see them*
*Spiritualizing me*
*I was afraid to begin*
*looking from within*
*but now I do see*
*I write*
*so I Can BE.*